The subject matter and
vocabulary have been selected
with expert assistance, and the
brief and simple text is printed
in large, clear type.

Children's questions are
anticipated and facts presented
in a logical sequence. Where
possible, the books show
what happened in the past
and what is relevant today.

Special artwork has been
commissioned to set a standard
rarely seen in books at this
level and at this price.

Full-colour illustrations are on
every page to give maximum
impact and help to provide the
extra enrichment that is the
aim of all Ladybird Leaders.

Index of Contents

A Ladybird Leader
leaves

written and illustrated by John Leigh-Pemberton
diagrams at the end of the book are by Gerald Witcomb

Publishers: Ladybird Books Ltd . Loughborough
© Ladybird Books Ltd 1975
Printed in England

Plants — how they live

A plant needs water, food and air,
just as we do.
The roots draw up water
and some of the food
from the ground.

Dandelion

The leaves take in air
through tiny holes.
The leaf keeps part of the air.
The sunshine helps the leaf
to turn this into food
for the plant.

Flower

Leaves

Roots

Different kinds of leaves

There are leaves of many shapes and sizes.

Some are smooth.

Some are rough.

Some are prickly.

Some are hairy.

Stinging nettle

Peacock butterfly

Ivy

eaves are the food of many animals,
irds and insects.

utterflies lay their eggs on leaves.

aterpillars hatch out from these eggs.

hey feed on the leaves.

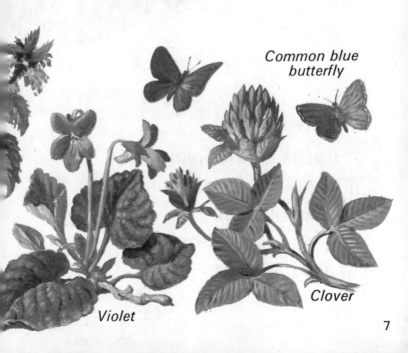

Common blue
butterfly

Clover

Violet

Spring leaf

Summer leaf

Bud

The tree

A tree is a large plant.
It grows in just the same way
as a small plant.
The leaves help the tree
to live and grow.

In winter, the tree is asleep.

In spring, the young leaves appear.

In summer the leaves
are fully grown.

In autumn, the leaves change colour.

Autumn
leaf

Winter bud becomes
next year's leaf

In winter the leaves of most trees fall.

A skeleton leaf

A leaf is made of
hundreds of hollow strips.

These are arranged like a net.

The large strips have smaller ones
branching from them.

The living leaf

The rest of the leaf
is made mostly of water.

Strong winds can dry up the water.

Trees that grow in windy places
have leaves like needles (see page 38).

Narrow leaves lose less water
than large, flat leaves.

11

Horse chestnut

Leaf

Young leaf

The shape of a horse chestnut leaf
is called 'palmate' (like a hand).

The flowers appear in May.

The nuts (conkers) ripen in the autumn.

They are not good to eat.

Buds
(sticky buds in March)

Flowers
(pink or white)

Fruit

Nut

The tree grows quickly.
Some are 100 feet (30.48 m) high.
Many are 200 years old.

Sweet chestnut

The sweet chestnut is quite different
from the horse chestnut.
The long leaves are edged with spikes
The flowers are small.
There are no 'sticky buds'.

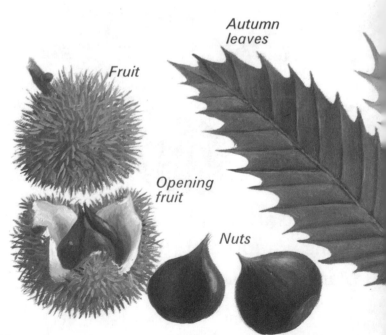

Autumn
leaves

Fruit

Opening
fruit

Nuts

The fruit of sweet chestnuts
is covered with bristles.
Inside there are about three nuts.
The nuts ripen in autumn.
They are very good to eat
when cooked.

Flowers

*Summer
leaf*

Oak

Summer
leaves

Spring
leaf

Young
acorn

Flower
(catkin)

Oak trees live for hundreds of years.

They grow very slowly.

The wood is very strong.

It was once used to build ships
and houses.

The fruit of the oak
is called an acorn.

Many animals and birds
feed on acorns.

An oak tree grows
thousands of acorns each year.

Acorns

*Winter buds
(next year's leaves)*

*Autumn
leaf*

*Oak
apple*

An oak 'apple' is a nest
made by a tiny wasp.

English elm

The elm is a tall tree.
It often grows in hedgerows.
The tough wood is used
for making furniture.

Flowers

Elm seeds have little 'wings'.
These help to spread the falling seeds
when the wind blows them.

*Elm seed
(enlarged)
There are thousands
of them every year*

*Seed 'cluster'
in spring*

Many elms die of
'Dutch elm disease'.
This is caused by a
fungus carried by a
small beetle which
burrows under the bark.

*The large tortoiseshell
butterfly lays its eggs
on the elm*

Apple

Fruit trees, such as the apple,
have beautiful blossom in spring.

The fruit is ripe in autumn.

Bullfinches destroy the buds
of fruit trees.

Bullfinch

Apple blossom

Apples

The wood of a tree
is protected by a tough skin.
This is called 'bark'.
If the bark is damaged
the tree may die.

Beech
(see also pages 8 and 9)

The orange underwing moth

Young fruit

Flower

Ripe fruit

Fruit

Nuts 'mast'

The leaves of a tree or plant
are called its 'foliage'.

The beech has very thick foliage.

The bark is silvery grey.

The orange underwing moth caterpillar—feeds on beech leaves

The underside of the young leaf is hairy

Winter buds

Beech wood is hard and strong.

It is used for making tools and chairs.

Beech seeds are called 'beech-nuts' or 'beech-mast'.

Many animals and birds feed on them in winter.

Silver birch

Winter catkin

Catkin (May)

Autumn leaf

Seed catkin

'Winged' seed (August)

The birch tree can grow in very cold places.

It has a silvery white bark which is very tough.

This bark is sometimes used for making canoes and tiles for roofs.

Lombardy poplar

The poplar hawk moth— lays its eggs on poplar leaves

Catkin

The Lombardy poplar grows very tall and narrow.

Like many other trees in Britain, it first came from another country.

There are six different kinds of poplar commonly grown in Britain.

Willow

The flowers of some trees,
such as the willow, are called catkins.

There are two kinds of catkins.

One produces the seed,
the other produces a fine dust,
called pollen.

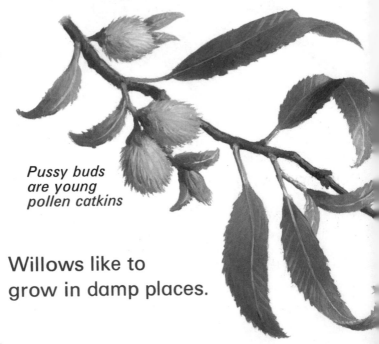

*Pussy buds
are young
pollen catkins*

Willows like to
grow in damp places.

The pollen is carried by the wind
or by insects.
Some of it reaches the seed catkins.
This makes them produce seeds.
These seeds fall to the ground.
From them new trees can grow.

Sometimes the pollen
is carried
by bees

Seed
catkin

Ripe
pollen catkins

Hazel

Unripe nuts

Winter catkins

Hazel grows mostly in hedges
or in woods.

It does not grow into a tall tree.

A hazel leaf feels very rough.

The pollen catkins appear in January.

They are called 'lamb's-tails'.

Seed catkins

*Pollen catkins—
they appear
before the leaves*

A hazel nut has a hard shell.
The inside of the nut
is called the kernel.
Hazel nuts are ripe in October.
Mice, squirrels and a few birds
eat them.

Mice open the nut by
gnawing a hole in
the blunt end ·

Nut

29

Sycamore

Spring bud

Flowers

The sycamore has very thick foliage.
Each leaf is divided into five points.
It can be about 8 inches (20 cm) acros
The leaf edges are shaped
like rows of uneven teeth.

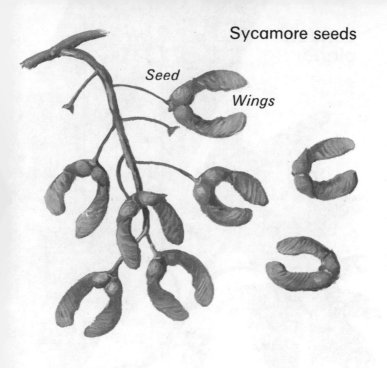

Sycamore seeds

Seed

Wings

Sycamore seeds grow in pairs.
Each seed is enclosed in a hard case.
Each case is shaped like a wing.
This makes it spin as it falls
to the ground.
In this way, the seed is spread.

London plane

*Young
seed ball*

The London plane tree is a mixture
of two other kinds of plane tree.

It grows very well in cities.

It does not mind the dirt and smoke.

Winter leaf

Seed

Seed balls

The bark of the
London plane tree
peels off in strips.

The trunk is left
with yellow patches.

The round seed balls
stay on the tree all winter.

Holly

Some trees have leaves on them all the year round.

They are called evergreen trees.

The holly is an evergreen tree.

It keeps its leaves for several years, then it sheds them.

Holly blue butterfly—
lays its eggs on
holly flowers
in the spring

Flower

The leaves are paler underneath

Berries in summer

Winter berries

In winter the holly has bunches of bright red berries.

They contain the seeds.

They are poisonous for us to eat, but birds like them.

Hawthorn

The hawthorn is sometimes called the May tree.

This is because the flowers bloom in May.

Summer

The thorns are hard and very sharp

Hawthorns are not large trees, but they make a thick hedge.

In early summer, the hawthorn
is covered with white flowers.
These produce the berries.
The berries are called 'haws'.

Greenfinch

Winter

The berries turn red in autumn.
They provide food for birds.

Scots pine

Red squirrel— eats the seeds of pine trees

Three-year-old cone open.

The long, thin leaves of pine trees
grow in pairs.

They are called pine needles.

They stay on the tree
for two or three years.

Pollen flower

Seed flowers

Young cone

Two-year-old cone

Winged seed

The flowers produce the fruit.

The fruit is called the 'cone'.

Inside the cone are the seeds.

Each seed has one wing.

When the seeds are ripe,
the cone opens.

Then the seeds float away.

Larch

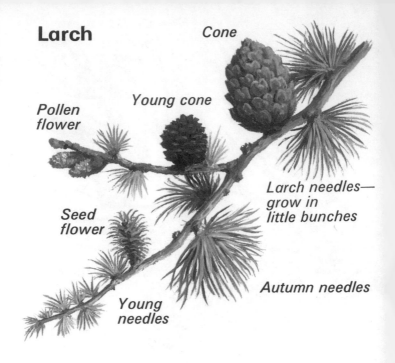

Cone

Young cone

Pollen flower

Seed flower

Larch needles— grow in little bunches

Autumn needles

Young needles

Trees which have cones
are called 'conifers'.

Their cones are made of hard scales.

The larch is a conifer.

It loses its needles in autumn.

Spruce

Pollen flower

Seed flower

Cone

Scale from a cone.
The cone holds the seeds.

Another conifer is the spruce.

It grows into a very tall tree.

It is the tree most often used
as a Christmas tree.

The needles of the spruce
grow all round the twigs.

Yew

Pollen flowers

The pollen flower and the seed flower are usually found on separate trees

The yew is an evergreen.

It grows very slowly.

Many yews are more than
seven hundred years old.

Once, yew wood was used
to make archers' bows.

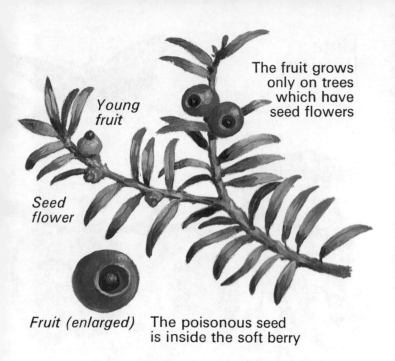

Young fruit

Seed flower

The fruit grows only on trees which have seed flowers

Fruit (enlarged) The poisonous seed is inside the soft berry

The leaves of the yew are poisonous.

Cattle and horses may die
if they eat them.

Birds eat the pink berries.

But they do not eat
the poisonous seeds.

Lime
(Linden)

The lime hawk moth—lays its eggs on the leaves of lime trees

Flowers in summer—often visited by bees

Lime trees are tall and graceful.

Their flowers have a strong, sweet sme

A drink, rather like tea, can be made from these flowers.

Bees like lime flowers.

Fruit in autumn

Lime trees lose their leaves
early in autumn.

The wood is much used
for making carvings.

Many musical instruments
are made of lime wood.

Whitebeam

Spring leafbuds

Flowers

'Beam' is the old English word for tree.
So 'whitebeam' means 'white tree'.
This is because the tree is covered
with fluffy white buds in April.

Chaffinch

Winter bud

Berries

Autumn leaf

These leaf buds are shaped
like little cups.

The flowers appear in May.

Later, they produce the berries.

These provide winter food for birds.

Ash

The ash is usually the last tree
to produce leaves in spring.

It is the first to lose them
in the autumn.

*Leaves
(May-June)*

The leaves are arranged in pairs.

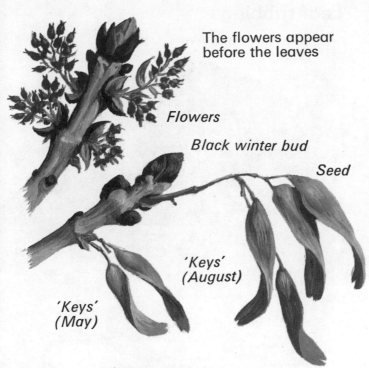

The flowers appear
before the leaves

Flowers

Black winter bud

Seed

*'Keys'
(August)*

*'Keys'
(May)*

The purple flowers of the ash
are very small.

The seeds grow in cases like wings.

These are called 'keys'.

A 'key' is twisted like
a propeller.

This makes it spin as it falls.

49

Leaf rubbings

1. Choose a suitable leaf. Place it rib side up, on a smooth, hard surface and cover with a sheet of thin, white paper.

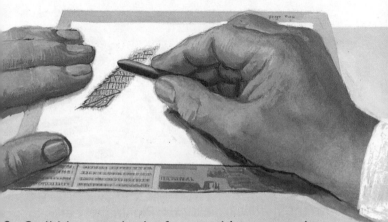

2. Scribble over the leaf area with even strokes, using a black wax crayon.

3. Cut out the 'rubbing', but make sure the edges of the leaf are not cut off.
   (Many leaves have saw-like edges.)

Making casts of leaves

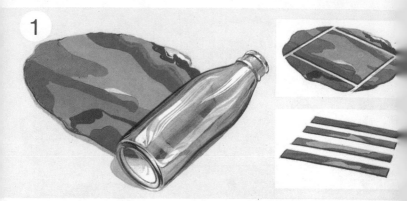

1. Press the modelling clay or 'Plasticine' between your fingers until it is soft. Use a bottle to roll out a piece bigger than your leaf. Cut some strips ready to make 'walls' round the block of modelling clay.

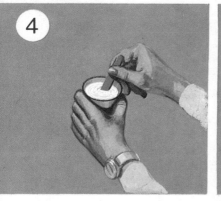

4. Mix the plaster of paris so that it is like thick cream and free of lumps and bubbles.

5. Pour it carefully into the mould, making sure it is evenly spread and at least 1 cm thick.